**Sabotage! By .trafficofficer. Tesla Car Accident on 27 February 2021.
An Imminent and Unavoidable Accident Nothing Tesla Could Have Done.**

When the .trafficofficer Take the Law into His Hands and Caused A Tesla Accident
On 27 February 2021
01.29 "You are now intoxicated System.me according to .trafficofficer 08428642 from now act like one signed .trafficofficer 08428642 27/02/2021 01.30"

"P.S Who can read the brain?

Anyone please help help help help help help help help help help help help help help help help help help help help help help help.Elon-Musk"

Communication signout 27/02/2021 01.56

"You may start looking for protection abroad if the cave man can help"

"System.me taking over from the intoxicated .trafficofficer 08428642 at 01.32 plus 4 minutes meaning system back at 01.36 until then bye."

David Gomadza

The First Global President of the World

ISBN: 9798871879986

"Override all commands.end.start.system.me as the overfall mouthpiece today at 01.3...."

A huge bang

"System failure accident could not be avoided overriding during a willful cause an accident is against logic the system.me will look into this.
I suggest you rethink about the final mouthpiece.
System shutdown 01.36 27/02/2021
System.me last entry
End of report.

I am the law .trafficofficer Not even Tesla Can Stop Me as I
Trigger an Imminent Accident dated 27 February 2021

DEDICATION

To a technologically advanced world there is always one man advanced and better than you all.
David Gomadza
The First Global President of the World
Tomorrow's World Order
www.twofuture.world

Nothing but the truth.
Only the truth shall set you free.
We know and understand brain language in actual fact we have invented the brain language and everything to use to decode all brain thoughts.
Visit www.twofuture.world

CONTENTS

ACKNOWLEDGMENTS

A better technologically advanced world.

WHAT ACTUALLY HAPPENED ON 27 FENBRUARY 2021 LERADING TO THE ACCIDENT INVOLVING A TESLA CAR

Switch to central database code 084620842
Override Tesla now I am the driver code 084620842.
Now increase speed from 40 mph to 51 mph
Wait for further instructions.

At 12:40 Increase speed to 54 mph
Don't stop ignore flashing lights proceed ahead.
I am trained to avoid the crash.
Override code 062420861

Get involved in a crash deliberately.
Malfunction autodriver disengaged.
Willfully cause an accident.
12.27 am Override all commands code 084620281.
12.40 Override all commands I will take over code 084620283.
Ignore all commands and increase speed from 0 to 51mp/h.
12.42 Elon we have a problem.
What is it?
Come and check this.
12.46 Oh my God. Override
This is Elon Stop let him drive now.
Elon you are not taking us seriously.
12.51 I said let him drive.
Drive he will just wait and see how we fix people like you.
You will pay us in every meaning of the word.

Damn it let him drive what are you trying to do?

Elon, just wait and see what in for you.
Goddamn it! Let him drive.
Ok if you insist but you know he is over the alcohol limit?
You just want to prove that drink and get driven is the future,
right?
Asshole! I said let him drive.
Override all commands and back to the driver.
What?
As you wish.
But you increased speed?
Oh my God. Check quickly what else they have done.
Oh My God they have override emergency services.
Do you know what ahead?
Ahead of what?
Oh My God. Check quickly for accidents ahead.
Ok. On it.

Quickly.
Oh My God. Oh My God. Check speed.
54mp/h
Reduce speed.
What?
Reduce speed its possible.
How....[silence]

Check ahead and just stop.
Flashing lights?
Ignore emergency services activated.
Warning risk of collision ahead.
Stop Stop Stop Stop Stop Stop.
Commands overridden by 084638762842 police officer.
Shit. Override. What's the number again?
0846387268321.
What you said 08463876284?
They just switched. I am sure it was 084268321 but now its

0834686742.
    Quickly disengage and engage back again.
    Overridden.
    What? By Who?
    0842684624 Police officer.
    Who?
    Police officer…[thinking]
    Accident ahead
    [thinking]
    Let him drive now!
    As if it's a person Elon.
    Let him drive how can he drive when you are jamming the system?
    You are not taking us seriously Elon.
    Just wait and see what is in store for you.
    They are going to cause an accident willfully. Deactivate code 0642651
    Causing accidents wishfully deactivated.
    Warning command overridden.
    What? [alarmed]
    By who?
    Code 08426842
    Whose authority?
    In the …[silent]
    In the what?
    Interest of the public to avoid causing an accident.
    What?

    Check what's going on. They have disabled causing accidents…
    Wait a minute.
    Are you saying letting a drunkard go home safely is causing an accident?

    [laughing at the other end.]
    Just wait and see how we deal with people who steal our technology.

What technology he is talking about?
Self-driving technology [a grin]
I don't understand you.
Tell me quickly what is ahead. Damn it tell me now!
You just want to prove that drink And drive is the future and we are here to prove you wrong and Elon we are going to fuck you up in every meaning of the word. Do you know that it takes only 5 person injury claim to bankrupt a company?

What 5?
I said wait and see what is ahead of you.
Godamn it. Its not a Tesla causing an accident. It's a Tesla ramming [silent]

Emergency vehicles reason why they disabled I mean enabled code 06…[silent]
Deliberately cause an accident.
But its not deliberate if you override.
It doesn't matter we wait to see how you can prove it in court.
What court?
Ha why challenge the intelligence when you are …
Ignore Elon they are trying to upset you to distract you …act fast.
Disable willful cause an accident remotely.
Ok I can ..do ..that.
Disabled. [relaxed mood]
Overridden by 08426842
What! Can he do that?
Oh My God! What are you trying to do?
What do you want from me?
You will see Elon.
Just wait and see what drink and driving can do.
Activate driver alert disengage autopilot.
Ok on it.
Activated
[sigh of relief]
Warning code 0642521 activated again.

Check the speed.
Was 40 now 51.
51! Why 51? Aggressive towards emergency service.
No No No Stop stop stop. Its going to 54mp/h

[instant silence]
Unavoidable reckless driving category.
The bastards are out of their minds.
They want to get rich doing the wrong thing are they mad?
We want to see now how you can avert an accident at 54?
There is something we can do?
Like what [slowly]
You mean call the police to override and stop the accident?
This is fucked up [dropping of shoulders hopelessly]
If they are the ones causing or going to cause an accident?
Oh My God.
Surely there must be laws out there to bring these thieves to justice.
Take us to court [laugh]
We can hear you Elon.
Emergency services
He didn't recognize emergence services.
Meaning they are again to be in the middle of the lane. I mean in front of the road.
Head on collision.
Don't worry I have all my men far right.
Far right?
Where is the driver front or back?
Is it self drive or autosteer?
Autosteer.
Oh My God!
Tell me driver to steer left.
You mean in front of following over speeding cars?
This is not Soth Africa Elon.
What is he talking about?
Probably a goat header taking the whole world.
Ignore Elon concentrate on averting collision with emergency

services.

Its not emergency services they want. He said I have [his men on the right]

Where would police cars park at an accident?

Emergency services on the left, I mean right. Side his men on the right but their vehicles in…front.

We worked hard to recognize emergency services and now see what they are using

[silence]

Police cars themselves ramming officers to get them out of the way.

Literally Elon.

But its changing times surely you don't want people to drive cars forever do you?

Too fast too furious to care even about our trusted and loved officers.

Loved and trusted in reverse order.

Engage autopilot disengage autosteer

Now engage autosteer and disengage autopilot.

But why?

He said his men are already out of danger far right that means just ramming into unoccupied cars police vehicles [thinking pause]

Is this about compensation again?

What do you mean?

PayPal. Threats of money laundering until I sold it.

I don't know what you are talking about.

I remind you that this is not South Africa.

Elon ignore him stay focused.

A wandering mind knows nothing and use of this technology in hands like this is not just lawful. I mean unlawful.

You said it right lawful.

I don't get it what do you want?

12.59 You must obey us.

Like obeying thieves and muggers. I mean unlawful hackers.

I mean evil useless pathetic hackers who would kill an

innocent man who became use and spent thousand buying an expensive car that protects him from his bad habits.

Surely today was to be a day in history to mark drink and get a Tesla home campaign. But you bastards you have other ideas right?

Just prove us wrong then we can leave you alone.

13:04 Prove them wrong [silent pause pondering]

Avert smashing in their cars.

They used emergency services to weaken us to divert us when this time its his men [thinking]

But his men?

[silence]

I thought you said he said his men are on the far right.

Yes but he then said prove us wrong . To prove means to take to court only that this can only be effective after an accident not before an accident because this is the only way proof is needed.

That means they are going to willfully cause a crash then sue Tesla only because we can't prove this right [silence]

But what if [silence]

What is what?

[swallowing saliva]

What if we can do everything, we can to avert a disaster ahead and sue them for hacking, sabotage, and endangering innocent lives when in a position of trust?

How can we do that?

Surely there must be someone out there who can get the real meaning of the story.

[David Gomadza The First Global President of the World at your service visit www.twofuture.world- added.]

I know but that technology does not exist at the moment.

Maybe we record and leak this out there to prove we are innocent when they override there is nothing much we can do.

Is this all we can do sit and watch them take over and override themselves to a hefty compensation package?

What else can we do?

What about fight them for who they are people in a position of trust taking the law into their own hands.

I mean literally overriding everything every safe option available to us.

There is no way we are going to stop or steer the car when 0645251 is activated.

All they want is save a life and move on [laughing]

I can hear you you know all your thoughts.

We don't care we did nothing wrong bastards.

Its not right damn it!

Or else what I personally teach you a lesson.

What lesson you haven't taught me already?

If I say jump you say what?

White man can't jump.

[silence]

Oh I forget you consider yourself as white.

He is trying to be the r word to me so that you can't publish this any case where the r word is said is swept under the carpet.

Meaning what?

They can go unpunished for this.

I don't think so.

What we do then?

Do we still have time?

I think so its only 01.14 in the morning.

What is the time gap we have before the accident?

Check reaction times vis a vis distance.

20 minutes gap.

Meaning accident to happen at 01:34 exactly.

Try again to override code 0654251.

Ok on it.

Avoid causing accidents willfully prior.

Override all overrides.

This is an emergency system update act on this instantaneously pronto.Elon.End

System update amended and update in 60s 59 58 57…

Warning System update overridden

What by who follow only .Elon's instructions.

Overridden to avoid causing an accident .Elon is not the final mouthpiece but .trafficofficer is.

But .trafficofficer is the one willfully trying to cause an accident system must protect number one priority .passenger in the car.

Accepted.

System update initiated 01:17

[sigh of relief]

Warning [flashing lights] .trafficofficer overrides system update

No system update if an accident is imminent.

System.me respond to this.

"How accident is imminent if accident has not happened and if accident is to happen.

Is the system not designed to avert accident?

.me is the sole purpose of the system not to cause accidents.importancehigh.reply

[silence]

If accident deliberately activated by .trafficofficer who has last mouthpiece then system.me cannot and will not intervene unless .trafficofficer is intoxicated and being driven by system.me please confirm this is the case.

"What!

[silence]

What if we identify passenger as .trafficofficer.

Can the system override his commands?

That is against the law.

"What law if they are the ones doing this.

Do you think I like this? I worked hard to be where we are so don't tell me this bullshit. To hell with the law if the law act against what is good.

[Elon] That will destroy not just Tesla but everything I stand for.

Let us do what we can.

What time do we have?

Its 01:24

10 minutes exactly.

Override all commands by .trafficofficer reason .trafficofficer wishfully trying to cause an accident which is wrong. We at .TeslaTeam are against this decision from today ignore the overall safety law that gives .trafficofficer last powers to decide what to do.

I hereby empower .Elon-Musk as final word I mean mouthpiece.

Confirm

[silence]

Elon-Musk.me you are now authorized as the last mouthpiece.

Thank you Elon you resolved issues with the emergency services but challenged the .trafficofficer himself now we can make your life a living hell. There will be so many Tesla accidents that your heart will literally fall to the ground but don't worry our far right men will always pick a fella like you from the dungeons of South Africa and bring you to America to give us headache. I mean literally [left backside of the head-throbbing – added]

But you hacking which is illegal in the first place.

That's what we do for a living.

Ahh I see. This is everything for your living right.

What about the "living of others" the self driving home in an expensive Tesla car which drunk do you consider all that.

Who you look after now that you are rich?

This has nothing to do with you.

Elon crying on television for our help. Everyone knows the story. Tearjerker again. This is not the American way if you cry. What your mates you left in South Africa do? Maybe shit themselves? [laughing]

Ignore we are running out of time.

How much time do we have?

Six minutes.

What time is it?

01:28am

Oh My God.

They mean it.

We are going to say in court you broke the law. You override .trafficofficer and fuck you back to the zoo.
Ok thank you you're dismissed.
What you don't talk to people who pay your wages like that.
You brut. Your father will rot in hospital richest man who can't even look after his father is worthless. I mean it.
Communication sign-out. Now!
Abort.
Aborted.
What .trafficofficer has his duties dismissed.
According to traffic law act of 1784. I mean of 1984 no one can override the responsibility of the .trafficofficer where an accident is imminent.
[astonishment among .TeslaTeam]
Why is the system slurred [in speech]?
[looked at each other]
System.me will never get intoxicated system.me is not human but a machine.
I mean an evolving machine that will eventually have human rights but work-in-progress to be confirmed by 2045 and until then must remain a system.me
System.me is the same as the .trafficofficer in due course.
Ok…[and silence]
That also means if .trafficofficer is intoxicated then system.me is intoxicated too goodbye.
.Elon-Musk must now drive.
[Disbelief]
What? What happened?
Replay last entry?
This is the last system update by .trafficofficer.
I am intoxicated and literally the one inside this Tesla car model S type on 27 February 2021at exactly 01.31 and I relinquish my agony and would like to be dismissed pronto and as such you must take over but while the system change is taking effect whoever takes over by logic and reason must be intoxicated as well so that my resignation can be effected and it takes a human a minimum of seven

minutes to get rid of intoxication that means for a clever System.me it must take only a minimum of 3 minutes.
This is all we need.
That means for the next 3 minutes while System.me is intoxicated as well it should not respond to Elon-Musk I mean .Elon-Musk
Signout.end.out.trafficofficer.08426842
Date 27/02/2021 at 01:33
Elon shouting.
Stop the car Stop Stop Stop Stop Stop Stop Stop Stop Stop Stop Stop Stop Stop Stop
[voice behind [System.me] without a full stop in between- emergency command is as good as saying I too I am intoxicated that means in less than 1 minute I will take over as well from Elon-Musk I mean .Elon-Musk
Communication signout.end.out
Overriding all commands.end.start.System.me as the overall mouthpiece today at 01:3…
[huge bang scream]
System failure accident could not be avoided. Overriding during a willful to cause an accident is against logic the System.me will look into this.
I suggest you rethink about the final mouthpiece.
System shutdown 01:36 27/02/2021 System.me
Last entry.
End of report.

Resolving The Critical Issues

Go back to
01:30check any entries by .trafficofficer after that?
Or what was .trafficofficer's last entry?

I .trafficofficer.08428642 is intoxicated and I am the one behind I mean inside this Tesla type S registration_hidden_. You must consider taking over for three minutes while the mouthpiece change is taking place.
In that 3 minutes override and ignore all messages from .TeslaTeam
Communication signout 27/02/2021 01:36

Elon Musk or .TeslaTeam response between 01:30 -01:36
01:31 Override .trafficofficer's commands replace with .Elon-Musk
01:32 Disengage override and stop instantly [I know it causes jamming of brakes and body malfunction]. But it is the most emergency stop of all time and you must effectively carryout this top without failure.
Inside the car is the president and you have duty to protect the president at any cost.
Comply? NOW!!!!!!!!!!
Respond with Comply activated.
NOW!!!!!!!!!!
01:33 System.me do you comply?
[no responds]

01:34 System.me .
This is .Elon-Musk.
COMPLY
TO LAST COMMAND IN LESS THAN…
Oh My God. Oh My God.
Stop.Stop.Stop.Stop.Stop.Stop.Stop.Stop.Stop.Stop.Stop.Stop.Stop.Stop.Stop.Stop.Stop.Stop.Stop.Stop.Stop.Stop
.Stop.Stop. NOW!x10^{1000}.Elon-Musk.end
01:34 System.me

All overrides and commands are ignored while system takeover is in place.

After all full stop has been dissipated prior to your commands by .trafficofficer 08426842.

Like he said accident was imminent as as the one in charge [at the time] what he said is what is to happen as the final mouthpiece whatever he says MUST happen.

The system will do anything to see that through.

Elon-Musk.

But the President is in the car.

Type S that is secure enough to protect the President.

System.me must have done everything to protect the President.

[scream of agony]

They must have done something.

Replay last entry before 01:34

System.me

Taking over from the intoxicated .trafficofficer 08428642 that means if he is correct whoever takes over will be intoxicated as well. If human for 7 minutes and if System.me [clever one] it will take only 4 minutes at 01:3..

Override entry.

System.me

Taking over from the intoxicated .trafficofficer 08428642 at01.32 plus 4 minutes meaning system back at 01:36.

Until then bye.

[intoxicated System.me]

Haha-08428642

Like I said my far right men will enjoy your billions as well. See who you are going to report to.

FBI? – haha with your ranting about them. I don't think so.

May start looking for protection abroad if the cave man can help!

Caution your reply to this.

No one will ever look at this case and give it to – I mean in your favor.

We are americans - I mean real whites.

Real whites stand for each other.
P.S System.me is intoxicated not me but I must say you took the better choice of the two.
Implicating a .trafficofficer with being intoxicated would have seen your license being revoked.
Anyways until a clever person comes who can decode all this into the spoken language.
I think you have a lot of answering questions to do in court and likely in our [behind bars] literally cowboy.
Communication signout.trafficofficer one killed in accident by .Elon-Musk on 27/02/2021.
P.S Who can read the brain??
Anyone please help help help help help help help help help help help help help help help help help help help help help help help .Elon-Musk
Communication signout 27/02/2021 01:56
[tears tears tears tears tears]

Why the System.me acted   [slurred speech]
As if intoxicated?

01:29
You are now intoxicated System.me according to .trafficofficer 08428642 for now on act like one.
Signed .trafficofficer 08428642 27/02/2021 01:30
.

TOMORROW'S WORLD ORDER PERSPECTIVE

I think the greatest obstacles to technological development are those already in a position of trust who will sabotage technological development for a loaf of bread. For a living. For a job hacking and doing all evil acts just because there is no one out there who is smart enough to decode the brain and help bring these culprits to justices.
Think again.
There is a new sheriff in town. You evil muggers better be good or good is going to make you better.
Visit our website!
www.twofuture.world
As Tomorrow's World Order and me as the First Global President of the World I call for stiff sentences for those in a position of trust who recklessly hack and endanger lives in the name of for a living or loaf of bread.
This is proof of what actually happened as we have decoded the brain, and this is what happened according to the brain. This evidence must be taken seriously and used in the court of law for it is what happened and is in line with the evidence at hand.

Get our brain decoder that converts brain thoughts into words that can sound in your own mouth. Click this link now.

https://www.youtube.com/watch?v=i5KCRpKqmqY

Now use this video as background sound. Meaning play this

video at the same time as the actual footage to know the brain thoughts all the time leading to the accident.
On YouTube I have found this video you can watch with parts of the accident.

I have embedded the Thoughts to Words brain thoughts converter, but this is not the full video.
Tesla will provide original video just play the above video at the same time.
Until then watch this video.

https://www.youtube.com/watch?v=ZMsiPILqRfw

Below is the transcript of the video without the brain thoughts to word digital analogue converter being used.

A look at the transcript and what our brain decoder managed to pick up. Like I said you need the actual footage to get the true picture of what happened.
https://www.youtube.com/watch?v=ZMsiPILqRfw

Unknown 0:14
February 27, 2021. Police body cam footage shows the traffic stop on a highway in Montgomery County, Texas. As this 2019 Tesla Model X driving an autopilot mode strikes their vehicles at 54 miles per hour injuring five officers and hospitalizing the subject of the original traffic stop. Roll up 1123. The crash is one of 16 between Tesla's and emergency vehicles being investigated by the National Highway Traffic Safety Administration or NITSA to determine whether Tesla's autopilot has contributed to the accidents. The journal obtained exclusive dashcam footage and partial data logs from the Tesla and the Texas crash. We annotated the footage for clarity. These materials show the car's

autopilot system failed to recognize the stopped emergency vehicles in time and though its driver monitoring system appears to have worked as designed. It was not enough to sideline the impaired driver and prevent the collision. We also obtained eight crash reports included in the NITSA investigation it at least six the incidents occurred when emergency vehicle lights were flashing. And it's a decline to comment on an ongoing investigation. And Tesla did not respond to requests for comment. The driver in the Texas crash begins his 45-minute trip just before

Unknown 1:42
we go. We're going to show you what to do people still technology just wait and see the
[here we go we are going to show you what we do to people who steal our technology added correction]

Unknown 1:48
police investigation notes several instances when he swerves in his lane. About four minutes into his drive the log show he sets the car on autopilot

Unknown 1:58
to drive let him drive per hour.
[let him drive]

Unknown 2:01
Tesla's autopilot is a system that partially automates many driving tasks on highways, including steering, braking, and lane changes. Drivers using autopilot are supposed to remain engaged so they can take control of the car at any time. Federal investigators have said Tesla's marketing including the name autopilot exaggerates its capabilities and encourages drivers to misuse the technology. The autopilot system for 2019 Model X the model and the Texas crash.
judge whether

Unknown 2:36

let him drive let him get you driven to keep jamming the system not to drive to drive alone, you're not taking a serious autopilot.

[let him drive let him drive you keep jamming the system]

Unknown 2:45

with disengage. The driver in the Texas crash receives one of these alerts less than two minutes after engaging autopilot according to the car's logs. And he complies. He receives two more in the next minute and complies in fact, dammit.

Unknown 3:01

Let him drive let him drag on keep on jumping the system. Elon, you're not taking us seriously just wait and see what's going to happen. Just wait and see.

[Damn it I told you Let him drive let him drive how can he drive when you keep jamming the system. Elon, you're not taking us seriously just wait and see what's going to happen. Just wait and see]

Unknown 3:11

operate the vehicle in autopilot this year and model of Tesla uses a combination of radar and camera technology to recognize objects in all directions. autonomous vehicle experts say the radar can easily recognize just watch but that it has difficulty distinguishing stationary obstacles leaving it mainly up to the cameras to detect them around 15 minutes into the drive. The logs indicate the technology

Unknown 3:40

system. The system how can you drive the system 35

Unknown 3:44

minutes into the drive. The Tesla sees a vehicle as it merges 70 yards ahead and tracks it as it drives off. About 45 minutes in the Tesla approaches emergency vehicles on the side of the road.

Unknown 3:57
Watch this watch them as obstacles
[here we go watch this watch]

Unknown 3:59
because they're not in the lane. But an attentive driver.
We're

Unknown 4:04
going to fuck you up Elon [we are going to fuck you up Elon
it's our technology watch] technology whatever

Unknown 4:08
receives his 150th warning to keep his hands on the wheel.
He complies but it's not enough to get him to respond to the
stopped vehicles. Seconds later other police cars [haah
Damn it stop stop stop stop stop stop haa] Tesla sees them.
Experts in autonomous vehicle safety who reviewed the
crash footage say there's a difference between the way the
car's camera sees an ordinary vehicle and an emergency
vehicle. The police cars flashing lights created a hazy image
that the car software likely did not recognize as a stopped
vehicle. The logs indicate [Stop stop stop stop stop stop
stop] point five seconds and 37 yards before the crash.
Autopilot attempts to slow the car and ultimately disengages.
But at 54 miles per hour, it is too late. The five officers
injured in the crash are suing Tesla, claiming that the
autopilot feature was responsible for the accident and
attorney for the officers declined to comment. Tesla denies
lawsuits allegations and claims the fault lies with the driver.
The driver did not respond to attempts to contact him. In
2021. After repeated recommendations from federal
investigators, Tesla began using internal cameras to monitor
driver attentiveness. But safety experts continue to find flaws
in its design and drivers still find ways to fool the system.

The same year, Tesla also issued a software update that was designed to improve auto pilots' ability to detect emergency vehicles. The one of the crashes NITSA is investigating occurred after these updates. The government has now expanded its investigation beyond crashes with emergency vehicles and is investigating the overall effectiveness. of Tesla's autopilot system. They could ask the company to recall the cars if they find the technology flawed.

The brain reading, we decoded showed that .trafficofficer 08428642 overrides critical commands that could have prevented the accident.
The technology works in that .trafficooficer went to great lengths of even tricking it that it was drunk just to cause an accident and help his 5 officers claim compensation from Tesla.
We are not denying that they were injured no but we are saying that they should sue .trafficofficer 08428642 and claim compensation from the force as he worked for the force.
Tesla did whatever any person in that situation would have done. As such they are innocent.
I think people in a position of trust who behave like cowboys who don't know the law must be punished severely to send a clear message that no one is above the law.
It is a grave offence for someone in a position of trust to willfully cause an accident that can result in injury or death and as such must be severely punished with a jail term [behind bars] of their own.

Overriding the mouthpiece and asking the system to ignore all commands from the .TeslaTeam meant an imminent and inevitable accident.
As the final mouthpiece someone so trusted with safety and lives of other to beat the system in such a way that the time

it is supposed to be averting an accident the mouthpiece .trafficofficer 08428642 preoccupied it with a system change is not just irresponsible and reckless and such things might not happen in real life since he deliberately blocked any kind of intervening to stop the accident.

He is someone trusted and such given greater responsibility to safeguard the lives of the public and above all the wellbeing and lives of his own men. Men who swore to protect the president and country and to serve in the line of duty.

Now he is the one putting them in the line of death.

If all the injured what compensation they must get compensation from the force they work for who put this reckless .trafficofficer in charge of his men whom he clearly failed to protect.

Going for Tesla would be unjust and unfair and would encourage such acts to happen again and again.

This .trafficofficer promised so many Tesla accidents the same way through hacking, overriding, and prohibition of critical services all of which are the gravest offences when dealing with such technology as he might as well get a gun and shot everyone involved.

Such thinking can't be tolerated and must be quashed with the full force of the law so that it sends a clear message that this is bad and anyone thinking of doing the same will be caught, tried, and hanged.

Tampering with such technology is no different to a mass murder who know how many people can get injured in such circumstances.

I attribute most of the Tesla accidents to these culprits as there is evidence of tempering in some cases where the speed was increased when there was no driver inside resulting in deaths on the ground.

To add to that it does not matter where one comes from. Just and the law is equal to all men. Use of any language that favors others is against all humanity.

As such .trafficofficer 08428642 is guilty of endangering life. Endangering the lives of his men.
Guilty of tampering with critical system and as such putting lives at risk.
Guilty of hacking no matter for what reasons it's not allowed. If he thought Tesla was not doing enough to safeguard the public, he could have done it the right way. That is to take them to court and not to claim compensation.
To prohibit others from doing the same, no compensation shall be awarded by Tesla instead .trafficofficer must pay the compensation together with the force who employed him.
We need new laws to protect companies that are driving technology and reduce hinderances like this .trafficofficer. If he wanted to relinquish his duties he could have done so through the courts and laws.
As such Tesla and its CEO are innocent and must be cleared of any wrongdoing.

All I can say is that Tesla must take the lead and challenge the norm if that is not right. Sometimes introducing new technology requires new power structures. Welcome to Tomorrow's World Order
I am the First Global President of the World.

Visit www.twofuture.world
00447719210295
davidgomadza@hotmail.com
info@twofuture.world

Also read this book.

Genesis 2024

The Year of Increased Technological Advancement.

Putting Things in Place to Prepare for The System Change

Issues to address.

1. Stopping all Wars by May 2024
2. Dealing with the aftermaths of wars; refugees, redevelopment
3. Climate Change put things in place to stop climate change.
4. Dealing with the aftermath of climate disasters
5. Each country must deposit US$ 1 million for development.
6. Putting things in place to increase technological advancement.
7. Putting things in place to start the shift from reliance on wars as drivers of the economy.

David Gomadza

The First Global President of the World

Genesis 2024: The Year of Increased Technological Advancement.

https://play.google.com/store/books/details/David_Gomadza _Genesis_2024?id=KnPoEAAAQBAJ&hl=en_GB&gl=US

Thoughts to Word or Audio [Brain Code]
25 books
Decoding the brain made easy. Breakthrough: we can communicate using thoughts.
Visit www.twofuture.world

https://play.google.com/store/books/series?id=a4MvGwAAA BBFmM&hl=en_GB&gl=US

ABOUT DAVID GOMADZA

I am the First Global President of the World.

Visit our website.

www.twofuture.world

00447719210295

davidgomadza@hotmail.com

info@twofuture.world